DRESSING UP

GILES L. TURNBULL

CinnamonPress

INDEPENDENT INNOVATIVE INTERNATIONAL

Published by Cinnamon Press
Meirion House,
Glan yr afon,
Tanygrisiau
Blaenau Ffestiniog,
Gwynedd, LL41 3SU
www.cinnamonpress.com

The right of Giles L. Turnbull to be identified as author of this work has been asserted by him in accordance with the Copyright, Designs and Patent Act, 1988. Copyright © 2017 Giles L. Turnbull
ISBN: 978-1-910836-57-6
British Library Cataloguing in Publication Data. A CIP record for this book can be obtained from the British Library.

Designed and typeset in Palatino by Cinnamon Press
Cover design by Jan Fortune
Printed in Poland
Cinnamon Press is represented in the UK by Inpress Ltd and in Wales by the Welsh Books Council

Acknowledgments

Alarm' first published in *Rockland*; 'Tomorrow's Dancers' was first published in *Poetry Wales* & 'Glad Rags' will appear in the Disability Arts Cymru competition anthology.

With special thanks to: Antoinette Rock, Jo Erbacher, Susan Nixon, Kevin Higgins and Mair DeGare Pitt for their edits, encouragement and support.

Contents

Alarm

Orange
the colour of traffic lights
that are neither stop nor go.
The bands of wasps
sandwiched recurringly between black
more electric than the shock.
Give me daffodil yellow
or the fathomless purple of night
as the orange sun's glow
begins to slow, then stops
before sinking out of sight
as we set the clocks
to wake us with a morning slap
for juice.

Wandering Eyes

After Helios

The world, at the extremities of sight
is like a rainbow
superficially flat
a slight curl at the edges
a vain cut to the cloth
songbirds in attendance
keeping dust and fingerprints off.

After all the paths
and the mazes
each one bringing you back
to the world of local councils
obsessing over speed bumps and high hedges
because we like to know what's going on next door
behind the glass and the roses ;
after the pubs,
busy from mid day to moon,
turn out at closing
with cold shoulder and a whiff of hops.

Then, tiptoeing obliquely
the kiss of another morning
like the rainbow reborn
high above rock and rubble
in one house can be heard
somebody is snoring
the sharp eye spies a man
shaving back the stubble
a woman applies her face
before lifting the latch
to slip out as the world awakes;
the smell of bread freshly baked
and the fishermen bringing home the catch.

Breakfast is the Most Important Meal of the Day

Effervescent green is the morning
oscillating with butterflies
flutter or fight

I am the coca cola Red Admiral
with skinny arms
iPhone white
it's tough landing a job
when you're uncomfortably skin and bone
behind a dozen anaemic replies

like being back at school pupating -
was my denim too faded?
was it not distressed enough?
A young girl
struggling to separate fashion from fears
even now am I too uptight?

Across the swanky table
the power suits
staring at me

staring at my pink shoes.

Tomorrow's Dancers

The future
flapping
like a flag in the metaphysical breeze.

The path, coiling like a spring
recoiling like a pistol.
the next step,

hovering beneath the feet
of tomorrow's dancers,
beginning in the mirror,

misty with the breath of getting-ready water —
the point where everything starts
and everything must stop.

An opened envelope;
the future
beginning with the windings of yesterday's clocks.

A Storm is Brewing

'Wake up! Paula,'
demands the wind with a smirk

casually whipping a bin lid
into a raucous flip flop down the street.

'Beat it!' I inwardly growl
submersing myself deeper between cover and sheet

eyes tightly shut
against the looming spectre of work.;

'Wake up, Paula,'
a whisper caressing my neck with seductive heat

'Make love to me
again, my sweet.'

Glad Rags

Oh yes,
these Versace trousers
are darling!
Can the legs
come up an inch
the waist out two?

Is that Dries Van Noten?
That embroidered v-neck
is to die for!
Camel hair, really?
Fantastic with a capital F!

What have you got
in socks?
I read in the weekend magazine
about cashmere socks
so delicate
they can't be washed;
will last 16 wears and then they're done ...
do you have a pair?

What time is it?
I really must
pick up a Rolex
if you've got a cheapish one -
a couple of grand?
Perfecto!

I think c'est tout
merci beaucoup!

Do I have a loyalty card?
I have a Tesco Clubcard!
Pay?
I was hoping to borrow these
on my library card;
No I don't have money,
I just came in
for a moment out of the rain.

Dressing Up

It matters
what you have on your feet
the difference between
underground weekend engineering work
and a system that does
(works)
not tied up
in a diversion of mazes
and replacements
step step
inappropriately in the wet
in flip flops
the colour of your shoes
pausing to take a breath
a vision, brewing from the paths
of percolating days
pacing out to the tune of fretting coffee machines
in the evening meets
as afternoon walks home
heading here in heels
in grey
your phone
you pause to answer
your toes.

Readers' Wi-Fi

Tell me what you see
on that screen
laptop dancer
crisscrossing connections
stripped of wires or ties
tell me where you've been
what's your history
your favourites
tell me who you've seen
in hotel rooms
in coffee shops
even a mile high
invisible electronic pulses
hooking up and hopping off
the beauty of the wi-fi.

Antipasti

Take the sights and the sounds
of the world, infuse
like a tea bag;
slurp.

I tip myself up
and words fall out,
like tortillas and snails
from my pockets.

A dinner party person
I am not,
mixing food and small talk
into something more complicated than hot.

Under the table
your foot touches mine;
it's a sign
in secret, we rehearsed.

Somebody Said I Looked Hot

(But of course, it is summer)

I wasn't made for heat such as this
searing herbaceous borders
like parchment
with cauterised scent;
pale bathers uncurling
from rainy retreat
into sanguine seekers of heat.

I was not meant
to languish under these naked skies;
July bleaching into August,
with fiery footprints
laid heel to toe
across beaches
and back to parasols,
while afternoon flagging strikes
the streets quiet, and on the wires
birds muster their faint energy for song.

The world and its everything
split to factions.
it's a war shepherding change
and all along
and in all the actions
its back is against the wall;
were it as simple to mend
as changing a fuse
or calling the medics
or putting down the guns
turning off the machines
and playing ball.

Mandelbrot

Words meeting worlds
spiralling
sprawling
spawning a myriad thesaurus points,
genociding a kaleidoscope of others
with a single zoom.

A glance
across the room
a breath of fractal romance
Julia *
amongst the leaves
blushing
like an ovum.

Dressing Down

Do you dream of knights in armour shining?
With this rose between my teeth
I turn my collar to the wind
and feign attack with verbal phrases
but seek no glory, so to speak.

Passing largely unobserved
into another morning
without a flag unfurling
without a second warning
and just this heart upon my sleeve.

A knight in ordinary coat
holds on to hope
in love believes
sharpens his pen
and quietly writes the story.

Turandot

Borrowing lessons learned and sharing what we knew
retreating into dream where needed; advancing
far into after hours, moments filled with talk
like shadows, nattering back and forth
and always spinning in dark and light
an enigma and a globe; your world,
the costume contradicting the fiery cold,
held time in abeyance; confronting fear and hope;
ruffled the morning chorus feathers before we called it day;
for who expects to sleep before riddles
just like these are laid to rest?
Losing was the only game to play.

All the Worlds are Stages

The curtain raised
you make your entrance
you pause and hear the audience. *Hush.*
At that moment my eyes are closed
and the present becomes an intangible fragment.
Because there is only me.
Because there is only you.
And because there is only everyone else.

Beyond that lie a thousand conceivable worlds
in every one a different beginning
and half have happy endings.
In half I open my eyes
in time to witness the birth of new life;
in half I surface only to see you leave—
your audience making their own ways home;
one ending differs from another only in the detail.

In seizing one opportunity, we know
one thousand doors,
one thousand other realities quietly close,
and at Fate's every touch we fall,
like two mortal heroes.

Sharp

Beyond this is a life
an easy come or often
easy go decision
creating storms from sorrow,
refracting prisms
building rainbows out of pyramid tears,
and every sacrificial piece
perchance to know;
to tear shards and shape
nightmares out of dreams,
living with
and through
and always because
of peculiar individual fears,
underneath the blackness
in every day and every year
leaving me as Pharaoh of a thousand secrets
in the seizure of a collapsing star.

Beyond this blanket shrouded world
smothered sometimes suffocating
leaking light like a dripping tap
through puncture marks that say
this is where it stops,
bringing second after second
inevitable as the next
as empty as the last

tick tick
tick tick
tick tock

but priceless
for I cannot capture even one single second
once the last is lost;
just wanting reason to give you
flowers not leave you
flowers for I would not know where to drop;
I could not put them down and simply go
not on my own,
always looking for you
in all that is in others —
as much as is as not,
for that is where you leave me looking
for a reason
to bring daffodils to an empty spot.

Four Walls

Pandora is here again
facing more deceptions
more lousy choices
a biscuit tin containing only crumbs
and a room full of noises;

Pandora's boxing
throwing left jab
counter punch
fighting for the championship
of the world between the ropes;
the crowd,
a lazy metaphor for hopes,
point and cheer;
a swollen lip
the ring, an irony—
the constraints of what we know
are where we feel secure.

Bored Meeting

Hands
painstakingly counted
and traced;
how many clocks
watched
like ladybird circles
on the windows of hot summer;
deliberated
points
drawn out
from one to yet another
and
slowly
but surely
eyelids slide
and shutter.

The Kapluna Effect

Light seeps in
dusting its knuckles on the smoky pane
hitting the walls
tessellated icy white
curved like a golf ball
gutted of its stringy elastic insides;
you can feel the warmth
an emanating promise
from the sleeping furs
a little matted
a little ragged;
outside the blizzard blows
it did yesterday
it will tomorrow
the bone-chilling wind,
restrained by caribou hide
stretched across the tunnelled door,
howls like a demon
rasping and raw;
at night the picture-house-like shadows
dance in the kudlik's glow
like ghosts taking fright;
and then the youngest says
'Aama, Mum, I wanna be vegetarian,'
and I'm like,
'And what will you eat child, snow?'

Little Faces We Still See

T-shirt on a line
wriggling in the rain
shivering in the snow

mitten marked 'L'
lost its string
baking in the sun
missing its bro

sock the colour of sunburn
hole in the toe

those that were not home
when the house burned down,
trying to pass on the stories
to those who do not know.

Ordinary Lives and Painful

How special is special?
What treasures would bloom
if every reflection came back
with stories fit to hold a room in raptures?
This would simply be another,
would only be a fact
and fancy would never flatter
ordinary lives, and painful
imperfections in the loves that matter
would never make them real or better;
every town
and every road
would never form a path tomorrow.
All is possible only when
fragile leaves a tattered
edge, like snowflakes falling after
mishap clouds have talked out pleasure,
and therein lies strength and character—
so much coming from apparent failure.